Northumberland
Estates

Burncastle

Broome Par...

GUNS
HG The Duke of Northumberland

The Earl Peel

Viscount Petersham

Lord Charles Hindlip

Lord James Percy

The Hon. Nicholas Soames MP

Robert W. Miller Esq.

Raisthorpe
Shoot

BEAT:	Hopes/Tollishill	
Grouse	322	
Blackcock		
Cock Pheasant		
Hen Pheasant		
Partridge		
Woodcock		
Snipe		
Duck		
Teal	1	
Pigeon		
Hare		
Rabbit		
Various		
TOTAL	323	

Date: 20th August 2005

GUNS

1   Lord Percy

2   Andrew MacKinnon Esq

3   Christopher Penn Esq

LINHOPE

...RSEUPCLEUGH

WEARDALE

FORNETH

REETH   DATE: 20 Au...

...dy Mary

Grouse:

Percy

Date 15th October 2007

Guns
1. Baron Eric de Rothschild
2. Sir Rocco Forte
3. Dame Vivien Duffield
4. The Hon Nicholas Soames
5. The Hon Rupert Soames
6. Hubert Guerrand Hermes
7. George Harvey-Bathurst
8. Rolf Sachs

...SANTS   205

...ISE

...KGAME

...DGE

Dedicated to my wife Lucy, to my brother and friends for giving and sharing such wonderful sport, and to all the keepers, ghillies and country folk who make life special. Particular mention for Northumberland National Park and English Nature for giving me the chance to fulfil my dreams at Linhope. Not forgetting the team at Fieldsports Magazine who were such a help in piecing this book together, and thanks too for some wonderful photography from Tarquin Millington-Drake, Bob Atkins, Charles Sainsbury-Plaice, Chris Knights, David Mason, Jake Eastham, Matt Harris, Glyn Satterley, artists Rodger McPhail and Andrew Ellis, and others to whom I am truly grateful. And lastly to my dogs, past and present who make it all worthwhile.

FIELDS OF DREAMS

A journey of sporting passion

Lord James Percy

First published in the UK in 2013 by The Sporting Library, an imprint of BPG Media   .

A catalogue record for this book is available from the British Library

ISBN 978-0-9574677-7-4

Printed in China
Editor-in-Chief Mike Barnes, Editor Jane Pruden
Book design by Alex Terry, BPG Media

The Sporting Library
Buckminster Yard
Buckminster
Grantham
Lincolnshire NG33 5SB
Email: info@thesportinglibrary.co.uk
www.thesportinglibrary.co.uk

CONTENTS

PART FOUR

The unsung essentials

Driven grouse at
Bolton Castle.
Glyn Satterley

The author pictured
with Connie, Pigeon
and Rosie.
Bob Atkins

CHAPTER TWO

Expectation is everything

LOVE IS... GROUSE

For the last century and a half, men have engaged in a love affair with the red grouse that goes at times beyond obsession. The king and queen of game birds, whose denizens stretch from the Derbyshire Dales to the north of Scotland, stirred the Victorians to build railways, roads and lodges, and moved generations of sporting and wildlife artists and authors to try to capture the magic on canvas and paper. The excitement, expectations and disappointments have in no way been lessened by the turning of two centuries.

By the spring, invitations – always hoped for but never expected – have mostly been sent out. True believers will already be questioning, wishing, hoping, guessing and soothsaying about prospects for the forthcoming season.

Records surrounding the enigmatic little brown bird are legendary. Back in the glory days before the First World War, entries of 50 brace butts, huge return drives and god-like marksmanship were commonplace. But I know that this is only part of the religion. There is a romanticism attached to the natural places where grouse live that appeals to the sportsman's spiritual side: the sweet scent of heather dust, sparkling burns, sweeping hillsides, huge skies and a comforting nostalgia in the knowledge that this has all happened many times before.

There rests a fear that this unbelievably special part of a wonderful sport, with all its history, all the people, the places, the adventures will not last forever if those against it eventually prevail. This fear in part has been responsible for a strong desire to show the massive positive ecological contribution that grouse moor management has had and continues to have in Britain's uplands.

This benefit is not just for grouse and grouse shooting by any means, but for so much other wildlife and for endangered species of flora and fauna. Grouse management has protected the peaty heather moorland that retains carbon and maintains the giant sponge effect at the head of catchments that is so important for the health of our rivers. The problem is that a large proportion of the general public who visits the uplands, and enjoy its rich biodiversity, really knows why the patchwork quilts of keepered grouse moor support this abundance of wildlife or why indeed the heath remains, compared to the vast swathes of grazed-out grassland or conifer forests. It is difficult to explain that the driver is grouse shooting – yet to reconcile the killing with the passion for the bird and all its surrounding glory is incomprehensible to those who are not involved in the same way.

But forget if you can, for a moment, about your smartphone, politics, money, mortgage and all the general trials and tribulations of human life and live a little daydream.

Imagine waking up in a beautiful shooting lodge far up a distant glen. You can't believe that the day has dawned, or that

Grouse in the heather.
Tarquin Millington-Drake

CHAPTER FOUR

Inspiration past and present

KIELDER CASTLE, NORTHUMBERLAND

In 1932, Kielder Castle, 12 farms, numerous cottages, a church, a motor garage and 45,000 heather-clad acres of Northumberland border country was sold to the newly formed Forestry Commission. The price was £150,000. The purchase was a flagship acquisition, a keystone in the drive to make the UK self-sufficient in timber, but it signalled the end of an era of sporting history that had spanned three centuries.

The 1st Duke of Northumberland built Kielder Castle as his hunting lodge in 1772. It was picture-perfect: a miniature fortress in neo-Gothic style, on a site chosen by his son. The 22-year-old Earl had travelled 12 hours from Alnwick to stay nearby, and had ridden over the moors the next day with a shooting party. The main purpose of the visit was to choose a fine site for the lodge 'for accommodating the Duke's family and friends in moor game shooting'[1]. You can imagine during an afternoon, Pompeii, the dog flushing out a blackcock, which had landed on a knoll. The party setting off in hot pursuit to find, when they arrived on the knoll, a spot they were so taken with that a bottle of claret was sent for and broken over the barrel of a flintlock, and the site for the castle was set. While much of the estate was originally purchased in 1373, it took another 400 years, and the popularity

of hawking and shooting birds 'on the wing' as muskets developed, for the owners to turn their keen sporting eyes to Kielder. Prior to this date, you were more likely to meet your maker there than a grouse as it was proper bandit country. However, from 1770 to 1932, Kielder Castle and the surrounding moors were to be the sporting domain of the Dukes of Northumberland. In 1790, a full century before the late Victorian and latterly Edwardian passion for sport, one Arthur Young[2] complained that moors were being bought up 'solely for sport' and 'thereby increasing their domain for shooting moor game'[3]. Clearly, grouse shooting was as much of a prized sport then as it is today!

As the art of grouse shooting evolved from the gentler days of walking-up and over dogs to the high-octane sport of driven grouse, so Kielder began to feature more frequently in the annual calendar of the Northumberland family. With the purchase of Balmoral by Queen Victoria in the 1860s the concept of ownership or leasing of a grouse moor, and the lodge life that came with it, became an accepted and socially desirable way to spend August and early September. The Prince of Wales loved shooting and the whole scene developed further through the turn of the century, even into obsession.

Living at Alnwick and owning vast tracts of moorland at Kielder some 40 miles to the west, the Duke of the day did not have to travel too far. As the numbers of grouse increased, so

Right: A shooting party at Kielder Castle.

1. Alnwick Castle archives

2. English writer on agriculture and economics

3. Alnwick Castle archives

Sir Conway   The Duke.   Mr   Mr. W. Orde.   Major Marshall.
Capt. Sturges.
Earl Percy.

more time was spent there. The roads between Alnwick and Kielder were rough but, by the late 1800s, there was a fairly comprehensive rail network throughout Northumberland, and there was a winding route from Alnwick to Kielder station. When the Duke wished to visit, the private carriages were coupled to the daily service (His Grace travelled in one carriage, the Duchess, children and whichever staff who had not gone on ahead, in the other.) Clearly the train was very handy and, judging from the 'how disposed' column of the game book, the stationmaster was well furnished with game. The entry for 29th August 1871 notes that the sportsmen actually took the train from Kielder to the far beat of Plashetts and shot their way home. If they wanted to go fishing at Countess Park, the main salmon beat on the North Tyne some 25 miles downstream, then the 10.10 from Kielder would drop the fishermen off at Redesmouth, a short walk to the river.

Sport, though the ultimate diversion, is a very serious business and particularly so for our forebears – the planning, expense and preparation was paramount. Until 1932, at the beginning of July every year, a team of stonemasons, painters, plumbers and joiners used to leave Alnwick for six weeks in order to maintain Kielder Castle, the staff cottages and farms, and to make ready for the Duke's arrival for the grouse in August. Two weeks before the Duke's family arrived, household staff would be sent over from Alnwick to prepare the house, linen, crockery and victuals, and there would have been much coming and going to and from Alnwick with wine, packing cases, guns, cartridges, dogs, fishing rods and all the other sporting paraphernalia required.

The moors themselves were good, but not premier league. Kielder is up on the watershed; its furthest reaches hit the Scottish border and are therefore very wet. The bags were modest compared to the top moors such as Wemmergill, Dallowgill or Allenheads, nor could they compete with the Angus Glens, or the famous Aberdeenshire or Inverness-shire moors. The record grouse bag in a day for Scotland was taken in 1911 on Roan Fell,

year' and 'you never know some might turn up'. Back in 1997 we had a similar, though less intense weather pattern and when we had a look in mid-September, having cancelled August, we shot 143 brace having expected a nice day of 50! But it didn't smell good this time. We took the decision – right or wrong – not to shoot until early September. Our neighbours at Commonburn, on the only other moor in the Cheviots, had, and that was our only ray of sunshine. Because, while not like the exceptional year they had last year, they have still done incredibly well, and there seemed to be more grouse showing up there towards the end of August. So maybe, just maybe there could be a wee few more at home than we expect... but probably not. We will find out on Monday.

For my long-suffering tenant, who has endured my woeful emails about expectations, his day at Linhope with his pals, is imminent. Monday 3rd September is our main event of 2007. The week before at Linhope is alive with activity. Milan, the Slovakian handyman, is concreting the road, cleaning the windows, raking the gravel, and helping the keepers with last minute jobs. Robbie the retired shepherd is cutting the lawns, strimming, bringing in logs and coal to the lodge. John and the rest of the keepering team check the butts for blocked drains, sheep damage to the turfs and any access problems. Endless phone calls are made to the lads in Ashington, the main source of beaters in this part of the world. If you had to go to war, pick an army of Geordies but just make sure there are no magic mushrooms on the battlefield.

The partridges have enthusiastically adopted their new habitats and are venturing forth in mini-feathered clouds to drink from the sweet waters of the River Breamish. The first days are barely a month away and all must be 100% ready by then. It all has to be totally spot on as you are only as good as your last day in the unforgiving eyes of the sporting commentator.

Time, this year, ran out way back. All those jobs on the hill and the roads were not done due to the wet weather: the diggers were grounded. Ritchie decided to go back to tractor work, so we were a man down. The one and only game crop failed in the main and generally, 2007 is looking like Her Majesty's *Annus Horribilis*, or as the Sun newspaper translated: 'Queen has bum year'. However, all is not lost, Linhope will rise again. Instead of sulking and wondering if we have not done enough or are doing something wrong, we will continue afresh to control the vermin hordes, to experiment with heather regeneration and to make long laid plans come to fruition. We must produce the very best sport, a blizzard of little brown rockets, so that our honoured clients might bestow upon the estate account a small token of their appreciation.

Preparations within the lodge for the shooting season have reached a crescendo, with Heather the housekeeper cruising like a Spectre Gunship at high altitude, capable of unleashing massive firepower. Linda and Jean, who come to help Heather, are busying and bustling. Richard the chef is briefed and ready to rock. Tomorrow is drawing inexorably nearer. Could there be some grouse? Just a week ago headkeeper, John was lurking in a peat hag at last light and he left a message on my mobile. 'No being funny or wishing to raise any false hopes, y'ken, but there's grouse calling all over tonight...'

First light – the morning of the shoot. It's a perfect day! Cool, overcast, with a light north west wind. By 8.45am nerves are jangling, bodies, dogs, guns and tackle are jammed into assorted vehicles. We decamp into a fleet of argocats. To walk would be fine but it would take an hour to make the first line of butts and we need five drives to make a decent day of it. I make a bid to pick-up in number four, manned by the Welsh wizard Jones, a well-known slayer of grouse. We waited and chatted. Jones is nervous, fiddling with his tackle, puffing madly on his Havana. Then there is a shout, and a covey of ten swoop down from behind the flank. He drills a tail-ender. Then a single cock drifts high and wide. 'I think that's probably it,' I said. Then a little group of three grouse come through. 'That's definitely it. Might as well go home now.' I knew it was no good, but hold on a moment, here is a covey, then a pack, and another.

Anyway, I could go on for pages describing the rest of the day. The Lord giveth, taketh, and then giveth in spades. I have never been more wrong, and even John looked somewhat surprised (though one might be forgiven for small suspicion that he didn't reckon on it being quite as bad as me). The total bag was 156 brace of the finest, fittest grouse you ever did see. This was the second best day on Linhope Moor in a history spanning three centuries. Huge credit to the keepers and yet you have to admire, even worship, in a deeply passionate and amazed way the heroism of those little brown birds. We have ridden an emotional rollercoaster that could possibly – maybe – be more disturbing than those early encounters with beautiful girls, when one's heart is not yet cushioned by worldly experience. Grouse are magnificent!

Happiness is being able to tell one's pals that their two days' grouse shooting in mid-September, are on. Faith has been restored and despite being somewhat bemused by our recent success, could it be anything like as good again?

The day dawned with another north wind – a stiff and very cold one at that, but we love a north wind at home. It means that we can get the grouse off the high tops and through the butts without too much trouble. Only seven Guns, but that included my brother Ralph, Eddie Norfolk, Francis Stafford, Sebastian Morley, Robbie Douglas Miller and John Dodd, which could be described as a tricky business if you are a grouse. I appear to have become the 'world's worst shot', and coupled with the worry of being the host, it was really six Guns who made the day. Final count – 151 brace: loads of grouse. And that was having opted to leave the big return from Dunmoor, the downwind end of the moor, where grouse from the earlier drives would have ended up.

The following day was a skirmish rather than a set piece battle. We headed out to the Black Butts and Bleakhope, an hour's drive across grassy hills in the Hagglunde BV306 tracked machine. This beat only takes five Guns as it is just a small island of heather, sandwiched between Kidland Forestry and the white ground of Ewartly Shank with no lines of butts but perfect peat hags to lurk in. Perhaps a few less grouse than last year, but still good enough to shoot 44 brace on another cold and windy day. Agent Jackson, a legendary sportsman, joined the squad, shot beautifully and nailed his customary five buns at lunchtime. Jackson (agents are still called by their surnames in the estate's office) gets so excited about going grouse shooting that I have only to hint a few weeks before that 'if' he wasn't busy and 'should' there be some grouse, we 'might' have a day on the such and such. One then has to confirm just the previous day, meaning only one sleepless night for our man rather than 20. That is true passion.

OCTOBER – A BUSY BACK END

We tried another day at the grouse on the main beat of Linhope in October but it was foggy on the tops with a south west wind and we never really caught up with them after the first drive. You only really get two chances at Linhope grouse before they go crazy and wild, and we had used up both of those. However, we had a grand day and shot about 30 brace. The highlight for me was that my little six-year-old, Thomas, came out – fully cammo'd-up – for the entire day. His commentary during the first drive ran something like this: 'Dad, why is nothing happening yet?' This was after about a minute of reaching our butt. Then he spotted a pack of grouse at approximately 600 yards going out across the flank. 'Dad, why didn't you get any of those? You're really rubbish, I got them all.' At last a covey swung down the line towards us. As I raised my gun, sure of a glorious right and left: 'DAD'! Thomas yelled at the crucial moment… 'Can I have my picnic now?' The covey sailed on unscathed. However, the beaming face as he went off to flank in the second drive with Wilkie, one of the flankers, said it all. That is probably it for the grouse season, although it would seem a little odd to go from 150 brace to 30 brace. Maybe we should have another wee look; maybe we should bank them. The old boys used to say: 'If you've got 'em shoot 'em, if you ain't, don't.'

Both partridges and pheasants flew well at the back end of the year.
Bob Atkins

On the tops they are flying like bullets.
Adrian Blundell

Meanwhile the engine room of Linhope, the partridge shoot, has been at high revs from the end of September. We've been a man down since July and John, Bob and Eddie have had their workload increased considerably with the shoot days, feeding partridges and pheasants and looking at the trap lines every day. It is a hectic time of year and the pressure is really on to deliver to our esteemed clients, and not just quality birds, food of course is of high importance and the lodge must run like a fruit smoothie. 'Pedro' Baxendale, *agent de chasse*, acquires and escorts a number of parties to Linhope and brings an air of military efficiency to proceedings. Both he and John are effortlessly organised and are more than aware that I am not really a detail man; left to my own devices, chaos would reign. As it is, my strings get a little taught at this time of year, at least until the main days are over and the shooting parties are 100% happy, so Agent Bax keeps the fuse on my powder keg damp, mostly.

The dozen or more days that we have had over a six-week period have been desperately still, and we are only really halfway through. The wind has only blown for two days but the partridges have flown well enough considering, and it has barely rained a drop (no good for the large stash of shiny new JP designed Barbour coats for sale in the lodge). There was only one day when the birds had no 'umph' at all, and that was still and bright with very high barometric pressure. Strangely, we have not been able to keep birds on north facing slopes at all. The result of no wind has been greater accuracy from the Guns, the stats giving 4:1 and 3:1 overall rather than 5, 6 or even 10:1 (bad news for home days after Christmas!). We are luckier than some shoots, but it has definitely been a bad year for the partridge men.

Possibly the best moment of this year was a day last week, down on a new drive at Ingram. The Guns stand at the bottom of a deep valley and the bottom flank push the partridges along the hill towards the top flank, then the beaters steadily bring the

64

drive over the valley. On this day, it was very still, you could hear a pin drop, and the partridges were very jumpy. From my spot on the top flank I could see them bouncing about in the bracken on a hair trigger. One of the Ashington lads had clearly had a big night on the beer, followed by a monster curry from the local Star of India. Like when Flashman's nervous bowels caused his horse to bolt, thereby precipitating the Charge of the Light Brigade straight into the Russian cannon, this lad broke wind with such force that it lifted 300 partridges, which picked up another 300, then another 300 straight back towards the bottom flank. 'Watch up, John, watch up!' on the radio, followed a few seconds later by 'Oh Shiii…!'

We have a new, and very experienced keeper, starting soon. Poor man, after his interview, which was on a shoot day and went fine, John and I pretended that we hadn't seen him standing nearby. 'John, what do you think?' I asked. 'Nah,' said John, 'Naid giud, nice enough but…' 'What no good for the job?' I reply, 'I mean, he's keen and he's very experienced? Maybe he's softened a pie or two lately, like me, but nothing we can't trim off him in a week or two, eh?' 'No, no he's perfect fae the job, it's just that I didna like his tie the dae…' Then we gave him the job. For three months now we have got the laddie, Dan, convinced that there are very dangerous wild pigs and huge boar at large in the woods. And so it goes on. One of our regular and worshipful loaders Davie Short managed to dye his hair a shade of mauve, not a good plan if you are coming up to Linhope. 'Hallo, Pinkie, what's gannin' on wi yer hair, man?' says Dave Miller. 'Looka, whaddyamean, like?' asks Shortie. 'Whey, it's all pink 'n' poofie like, y'kna!' says Dave. It then dawns on the hapless Shortie that he'd unwittingly used Mrs Short's special Henna shampoo.

The lads from this neck of the woods in Northumberland are quick, you know. There was one guest for whom nothing was right from the moment he arrived. Out of the shooting, sun in the eyes, not enough birds, too many birds, too high, not high enough, you know the type and his final whinge was that he was more of a pheasant man and not mad about partridges. Quick as a flash, and thinking about the only two pheasants seen at Linhope that day, his very fed-up loader said: 'Well, Ah' reckon yaz come to the wrang place then, pal.'

DECEMBER –
AN UNEXPECTED SURPRISE

The keepers had maybe two weeks to catch up on jobs, get Christmas out of the way and prepare for the first of the family days just before New Year. Christmas, Boxing Day and beyond, seem to go on forever when getting excited about a home day. The 28th December dawned with a proper gale, so much so that the Rabbit Wood – a scruffy acre of blown timber that is the world's worst drive – came into play and produced pheasants of such pace and drift that most sailed by unscathed. We finished with a nice bag of 80 for the day, but the partridge drives were worryingly quiet. Then came a couple of snowy days and the next shoot was absolutely fantastic with pheasants back in the woods and lots of partridges in the main drives. The snow did not affect the birds flying at all, surprisingly, and the second day was another gale with some really big high stuff. For the final two days I had a small, mobile and deadly team of killers. The instruction was a full kill order on cocks and partridges, which was properly executed. Perhaps the best moment was catching out a number of birds that had been sneaking out all year, both pheasants and partridges, in the Shank Burn, taking the drive halfway between the normal two drives. I think we shot about 70 head in the drive: some very high, some medium, some rather low – half the bag for the day and completely unexpected. Perhaps there is a good pointer there for loads of shoots where the drives are taken the same way every time they are shot. A little thought from the headkeeper, and persuasion to the boss to try the experiment seems often to yield a bit of a harvest.

More strong fliers
at Arundel.
Jake Eastham

food, chemicals, and constant predation. If you look at the refuge populations it gives us an even greater understanding.

The moorland fringe for example – keepered ground, reasonable habitat for nesting and cover, not much in the way of herbicide and plenty of seeds and insects in the wetter areas. Partridge coveys can reach as high as 18 or even 22 chicks but the territories are huge as food is scarce compared to old style arable in gentler climes. Numbers are therefore never going to explode like they used to in the lowlands. In addition, by their altitude, the moorland fringes have a coarser climate in winter and poor weather in late June and early July and by example in 2008 and 2009, and in the late 1990s, inclement weather almost wiped out the hill partridge in some areas.

There is, however, a wind of change... there is a small but growing number of shooting people who have a deep love of truly wild quarry that goes way beyond shooting. They have an understanding of the countryside and a true respect for the creatures within it, and a mindset which is a million miles away from the big corporate pheasant shoot. Not in a decrying way at all, just different. Now that ecology is not solely the preserve of the scientist, the understanding of the ways and habits of the partridge is being better understood all the time.

Not that this is ground-breaking news: Aymer Maxwell's famous book *Partridges and Partridge Manors*, written in 1911, gives 300 pages on how to best manage your manor for partridges and it is all there – nesting habitat, the need for open spaces for drying off chicks, the importance of cover against aerial attack from hawks, the need for winter feed and the chicks' sole dependence on insects. The difference was that in those days they had perfect hedgerows, loads of nesting, no chemicals, no vermin, winter stubbles and an army of keepers!

There is every encouragement now to provide habitat for partridges (as well as a host of other farmland birds) through Entry and Higher Level Stewardship. The farmer or landowner is financially incentivised to recreate, at least in part, the habitat that

81

Aymer Maxwell described, while still commercially farming the bulk of the land. It is the edge habitat which is key – a combination of four requirements: firstly, nesting habitat in the form of hedgerows, thick grass, bracken, or broom; secondly, chicks need bare places to dry off.

The third requirement is insect and seed-rich strips with mayweed, knot grass and other broadleaf plants which are the host plants to beetles and spiders and – the caviar of insects as far as partridges are concerned – sawfly larvae. The fourth is the crucial need for a crop to provide protection from hawks and buzzards, which both adults and chicks can scoot into at the first sign of danger, to be protected and hidden.

Environmental Stewardship field margin prescriptions by themselves are not perfect for partridges – the grasses get too dense, the insect-producing plants may be too high for chicks to reach and so it is up to the individual to identify the correct combination and provide as varied a habitat as possible. Conservation headlands with quarter rate seed application and herbicide that does not kill the broadleaf weeds is a key habitat when combined with good hedges and some aerial cover. Another imperative is supplementary feeding throughout the winter and into late spring. And, of course, the control, suppression, decimation of as many predators as possible: stoats, weasels, crows, foxes, rats and magpies should be shown no mercy. With no habitat and no food you will have no partridges; with good habitat and some food you may build up a reasonable stock but with a little (or a lot preferably) of keeping and good habitat and hoppers every 200 yards, then you will have success.

Needless to say it doesn't come cheap, it is a labour of love, particularly as you lose up to half your stock every year to pairs going off to the equivalent of the Green Zone in Helmand Province by emigrating to unkeepered territory and getting zapped by vermin.

There are a few shining examples to show that it can be done – at Alnwick, the Duke of Northumberland's headkeeper, Gary Whitfield, and his team have made a dream come true, more than once, with days of over 100 brace of wild greys from a starting point of possibly 12 pairs in 2002. Raby Estates possibly pioneered the comeback of the wild grey in the late 1990s, achieving days of 70 brace.

The GWCT's project at Loddington, set up in 1992 to research the effects of farming on wildlife and the environment has proved the value of the habitat, keepering and wild game relationship. The organisation now has successfully applied its techniques to wild partridges at Royston in Herefordshire. After six long years of building from scratch and the planting of seven and a half miles of hedges amongst all the other measures, the Duke of Norfolk's farms in Sussex showed an autumn count in 2010 of 1,200 wild grey partridges. One year later, in a howling northerly gale in early October, the bag of wild partridges (I think a few more English than French) was 298 brace: an unbelievable result. Quite apart from the sheer volume of partridges, what was truly remarkable were the clouds of little birds – sparrows, linnets, larks, pippets and finches amongst others on the farm, not to mention a beautiful marsh harrier, and the full spectrum of lowland birds of prey.

Above left: Greys in the stubbles.
Chris Knights

Right: Reared redlegs beautifully presented at Hillington, Norfolk.
Mike Barnes

CHAPTER EIGHT

Pheasants at Christmas

THE BOXING DAY SHOOT

Picture the scene for a sporting family on Christmas Day, 4pm. Mother is finally coming down from DEFCON 3 after weeks of present-wrapping stress. Father has eaten too much and wants to sleep or watch *Iron Man 3*. Young master wants to play footie, lassies fight over each other's presents and the wee man is blissfully playing with the cardboard boxes and having a ripping-fest in wrapping paper. Church was fine, the sermon was long and rambling and the vicar a little tight, which added to the festive spirit. Lunch was magnificent, the best bit being the chipolatas with bread sauce. The sprouts are making the little fellow fart, much to everybody's amusement. But all in all, life is good. Peace and goodwill to all men.

It is great to have all the family around: sisters-in-law, aunts and uncles, cousins *et al*. The only thing is, you are not really used to having them around and, much as you love them (one hopes), it is quite another thing them being in and around your space for days on end. In fact, it can be a bit of a shock to the system and very tiring having to be nice to everyone for extended periods of time.

So, our irreverent sportsman's thoughts turn to the Christmas shoot, a sanctuary of light in an otherwise dark tunnel of entertaining, washing up, and towing the wee man on his 'new red trolley'. It is tricky to escape *la chasse* even on Christmas Day as every other card is a cock pheasant standing on a yuletide log or a partridge in a pear tree. The shoot might be on Boxing Day, but more likely a couple of days afterwards. If you venture out on to country roads at 8am, any morning after Christmas, you will see very little traffic other than pick-ups and 4WD's full of spaniels and labradors. Well-built, ruddy-faced men behind the wheel, youngsters stuffed into the back.

Keepers, a little jaded after a couple of months of high stress levels with let-shoots and so on, have had a day or two to recover and bounce back with renewed vigour. The season has only a month or so to go, and the tension seems to ease – now the real sport can begin: outwitting cock pheasants, changing times of drives and feeding. Maybe even a week of hard weather to hunger the birds back into the woods.

On the fifth day of Christmas it is the day of the shoot. It has snowed a little a couple of days before, just a scuffing but the ground is hardening off with last night's frost. Whether you are the laird or one of his guests you cannot fail to feel your heart quickening as you emerge from the front door to biting cold, gravel crunching under foot, windscreens white with ice and rutted puddles frozen up the farm track. It is quite still around the big house, but up in the beeches there is a stirring in the topmost branches. The stars are still shining but there is a grey

The wily old cock. Painting by Andrew Ellis.

dawn far to the east and you can sense more snow on the way. You can hear the beaters and pickers-up parking their cars in the yard. It may have only been a week or two since the last shoot but somehow it seems a lifetime ago.

The days are still short so there is a slight urgency to be off, though the headkeeper just manages to delay the Guns time enough for the birds to make their way up to the game covers and woods. His stops are old hands. They know the form, quietly getting into position.

The house guests are ready for action. The local Guns have already arrived, had a cup of coffee and are booted and spurred. A couple of youngsters, fresh-faced and quivering with excitement check their gear and meet with their minders for the day – the latter all old hands, too: gentle, strict and encouraging. Eventually everyone is squared away into vehicles and the yard falls quiet as the last in the convoy disappears in a cloud of white exhaust fumes.

The first drive is Monty's Oaks – an open hanging wood on a hillside, full of brackens, elders and gnarled old oak trees. The wind is perfect; the early sun has given to steel grey. Our man on peg one reaches his spot, a little private nirvana just around the corner. The end Gun is at a point where once the beaters are passed, there comes the odd very high and very fast cock pheasant. He takes a deep breath, sucking cold air deep into his body, nods and waves at Bob the picker-up who is taking up position a couple of hundred yards back. He rolls a little smoke to celebrate making it through the dark times and concentrates on the job in hand – dog by his side – with plenty of time to savour the moment. He slips a couple of 32 gram VIP shells into the chambers and makes a couple of swings into the sky. He wonders how many times will that scene be played out across the nation, on big shoots and small, and over the centuries how many generations of sportsmen have thought and done exactly the same things.

Not too long after, a muffled shout pulls our man on peg one out of his happy reverie and there, way over the wood, is a hurtling, soaring, banking and very indignant cock pheasant. The wily old bird tracks too far left for a shot but not far behind him is another, less experienced one who takes on the gap in the trees, the nirvana. Our man has made him, is tooled up and ready. Everything is in black and white, or shades of brown but way up in the sky is a flash of crimson.

Four drives before lunch and just time for one after, if you don't delay. Lunch is in the barn, a cosy place where you can wear your boots, the stone floors are warm and the food is plentiful. Just before you start to get sleepy there is a call to arms for the final drive. You all walk out from the barn; there is free-flowing, easy conversation. Excited chatter from the youngsters who really thought that lunch was a waste of killing time, and no Blackberrys or iPhones to interfere. Onwards to Northcliffe Dean: a heavyweight of a drive and a prize venue. Loaded with monster pheasants and squadrons of partridge, it is the big one and never fails to deliver impossible birds. A heavy cartridge tally and a pitifully small body count makes for a grand finale.

Once again the Christmas shoot has come and gone: an institution rivalling its flanking nationals of Christmas and New Year - well in some of our books anyway. This island life – long may it last - with all its little sporting operas across the shooting field, at once insignificant to the vast majority yet to everybody who is there, entirely consuming. It is the fabric of country life itself.

Britain's stalwart game bird – the pheasant.
Chris Knights

CHAPTER ELEVEN

Salmon on the Tyne

THE NORTH TYNE –
A FAMILY AFFAIR

Every year, in April or early May, maybe once, maybe twice, my father would announce that we were to get our fishing gear ready first thing in the morning. A day trip was on to go to Countess Park – the family stretch of fishing on the North Tyne river. The old Renault estate would be fired up and parked up outside the fishing room at Alnwick. When all was ready my parents, my brother Ralph and I would set off on the 40 mile journey to the far west of Northumberland, turn down a rough track, along the old railway line and down through the oak woods that line the river. If we didn't get stuck on the way down, we definitely got stuck on the way back up, but in between times always unfolded the most perfect days. Cut sandwiches and paté, sporting and military chocolate, rain, sun, midges... the usual.

The hut, a Canadian-designed log cabin built in 1860, still stands above the most prolific pool. There is a table outside under a silver birch tree where you can sit and watch the rapids churn into the head of the riffle from the belly of the pool; foam and fleck on the dark peat stained water. The riverbed is knobbly with stones the size of toasters, a little gravel and some whopping great boulders. You can't see more than a few inches into the water but out in the stream you can see where the big boulders part the surface foam with the turbulence created by their bulk. It's a very moderate river to wade, at least in the middle stretches – something like trying to walk over a demolished building, through three feet of water wearing a blindfold and high heels.

There was one rule, and that was that we had to run through one pool with a salmon fly, just in case, and then we could go after the very numerous wild brownies. Fat, hungry, with golden bellies and pink flesh they came up to a Greenwell's Glory or a Purple Spider and fitted perfectly into the little smoker: sizzling skin, oak sawdust and purple meths burning away to form a delicious wafting aroma like no other.

A hundred years before, in the 1880s, the whole Tyne system of the South and North Tyne, with various tributaries and the main stem of the Tyne below Hexham, was overrun with fish. One hundred and twenty thousand salmon and sea trout were taken out in one year by estuary nets, river nets and rod and line. The Tyne was the most prolific river in Britain. But by 1950, salmon were virtually extinct, the industrial poison and raw sewage down at Newcastle was too much for the smolts making out to sea. Just a few would make it during a big flood, flushed out to sea on spate water.

For years no one from my family ran into a fish at Countess Park, nor did others fare any better on the great beats downstream: Chipchase, Chesters, Styford and Bywell. My father had caught one in 1929, and another in 1965. My brother had caught a 5lb sea trout in 1984, and my mother, kipping on the river bank had been woken by a big splash. Then, on a visit in September 1985 it all changed. I went to the Croy pool, a wide treacly glide with a Victorian fishing groyne built out into the tail of the pool. I was too lazy to put up my salmon rod. I had not seen a salmon jump in all my life there. I was out of sight of my father so I just tied on a Black Shrimp salmon fly to my trout rod on 2lb trout gut and cast out. The last thing I expected was a beast that as far as I was

Croy Pool at Countess Park – a Victorian fishing pier built out into the tail of the pool so that fishermen could cover the key lies.
Lord James Percy

concerned could only be caught in Scotland. As my fly swung round there was a great swirl. No contact. My heart was in my mouth. I couldn't breathe. To cut a long story short I ran back to the hut, put up my big rod and – first cast, same place – the line tightened and after ten minutes of playing and praying there lay

on the bank an 11lb salmon. What is more is that when I had been playing the fish I had seen a dozen others splashing around, the first returning progeny of the Kielder hatchery and a monument in burnished silver to Peter Gray who ran it. The North Tyne was on its way back from the dead.

For the next few years it was a glorious journey of discovery, a mile or two of pools, dubs, rips and glides, frog water and pocket water, overhanging trees and ripped waders. This bit of river, a good 60 miles from the sea, is hidden away in a steep wooded valley. It is neither a highland stream nor a lowland stretch, not a spate river, but it needs water. The stage describes that moment of late adolescence on a river's journey. There are hundreds of yards of white water rapids, cliff faces, natural sills of rock that look like man-made obstructions and pools called the Devil's Leap, the Diagonal and the Island Stream. New lies were discovered, kept secret for as long as it took to get back to base and tell the others. Fish were lost around boulders or tree roots; big ones too. The average weight is around 12lbs but there have been plenty of 20lbs over the last 30 years, even a couple of 30s. It took a year or two before anybody really fished the Tyne and so the salmon were beautifully free-for-the-taking. Basically, if conditions were right and you saw a salmon jump you often caught it.

One day, my cousin and I went to the river. We got there at lunchtime so I asked him to catch a couple of trout for the frying pan. As I messed about in the hut I heard a shout, which I ignored. Surely he could net a little trout by himself. Then another shout

Family photo... from left: Eliza, James, Sam, Tom and Willa Percy.
Above: Lucy and Eliza Percy.

– it must be a big one. I went to see what all the fuss was about and sure enough there he was, split cane rod bent double and a large salmon on the dropper fly of his very light tackle, refusing to budge. We did get the fish in the end, it was 13lb and the tail section went straight into the pan.

There was camping in the hut, cooking over the old wood burning stove, sputtering candles, wine, and smoking loads of those short Silk Cut. I remember sharing the night fire with Joe my dog and a beautiful raven haired girl with big hands who I had never met before (just the fire, mind you). On other occasions I would pick up my girlfriend from the train and spirit her away to this fairy tale place.

We caught fish after fish, each year better than the next. With Kielder dam and reservoir finished in 1982, the hatchery up and running and the Toon (Newcastle) effluent improving, the runs were increasing. The sadness was that my father never took another fish after the resurrection of the North Tyne but at least he saw a semblance of a run come back after 50 years. Another glorious moment was seeing my wife Lucy hook a big fish that took major exception to being interfered with. She had caught fish before, but only little grilse and she stood on the groyne, rooted to the spot in shock as this fish tore off 100 yards of backing in one go. 'RUUUUUN!' I shouted and she took off, but the pier is only 40 yards long and she ran out of runway. The fish kept heading for Newcastle and we could only watch as the last few turns of backing disappeared to just the bare drum. A moment of heavy tension, a thrashing tail 200 yards away and then it was gone. The long wind back of slack line and a piggy tail of nylon: no fly.

To the eye, nothing much has changed in a hundred years this far up the river. The landmark boulders never move; there is more vegetation growing on the banks as the effect of the huge dam 20 miles upstream has reduced the ferocity of the floods and ice. The trees grow higher. The only changes really are the names and faces. Robbie who keepered on Stanhope Moor, has retired again at the age of 83 and Gerald has taken over. For years, when my

children were too small to do anything near a river except roll into it and frighten the fish, the North Tyne became a bit of a distant memory. We lived too far away but my son Tom, who three years ago spent a week doggedly flogging the Spey for a week without a touch, caught a 4lb sea trout on the fly after only ten minutes at Countess Park. What a triumph to behold as it cartwheeled down the Salmon Stone pool. Below the hut you can line up a posse of flaxen haired little people armed with everything from fly rods to

The author wading for a daytime sea trout.
Inset: Thomas's first fish – a sea trout taken on the fly.

bamboo poles. It is fly only, but you know a spinner, the wheel of fortune, from time to time – pour encourager – is key.

There is something old fashioned about this enchanted piece of river; maybe because it is not hammered day after day like the Tweed or the Spey. It couldn't stand it. Sometimes pools may not be fished for weeks, and perhaps it becomes a refuge. There are different times of the year when things happen – never much before the end of April, but May and June are ideal for a silver springer. July and August for summer fish and big sea trout. Back end for volume and pools full of 'lunkers' throwing themselves out of the dark water. There have been some special moments, like a 20lb, an 18lb, a 14lb and a 9lb fish caught in four consecutive casts, and the day with a friend when we caught seven fresh silver sea trout to 5lb off the same lie in an afternoon. There was the sunny day when I had fished all day for not a touch and, timed to perfection as always, my brother turned up as the sun dropped behind the wooded bank opposite and proceeded to pull out five salmon on the trot. My cousin once caught nine fish in a day there, the day after the Foot and Mouth ban was lifted and the whole river hadn't been fished for some time.

While the return of migratory fish to the North Tyne is cause for great celebration, compared to pre-1900 it is still a shadow of its former glory. Seven miles of the upper reaches of the main river were lost to the Kielder Reservoir, and I would hazard a guess that maybe 80% of the spawning and nursery streams are also above the dam that has no fish pass. Whether billions of spruce and pine needles rotting in a vast expanse of cold de-oxygenating water is also having a detrimental effect on all salmonids is difficult to say.

However, whatever is going on in the river, whatever is happening in the world, the North Tyne at Countess Park[5] is a mystical silver stream in a folded corner of Northumberland. It is a place where you can go to fish a little, dream a little, and while away a summer's afternoon just like they did a hundred years before.

brand new tweeds, smoking big cigars whose equally smart and highly polished drivers/loaders have to carry their guns, cartridges, spare coats, satellite phones (and seats for God's sake!). I am sure that if this scene is becoming the public perception of driven shooting, especially when the Guns are the type who, when the drive is over, waddle back to their motors without a second glance at the slain, then it will all come to an end in short order.

How on earth our predecessors managed to do the business in the old days with the huge dinners and vast quantities of alcohol the night before, I cannot think. Even 20 years ago, the great house parties threw tales of shooting 500 brace of grouse after a night when no one got to bed before 5am and were still crazed with drink at breakfast. They were definitely more resilient to drink and late nights then, and on the whole we are lightweights now in comparison. Equally it must be a bit galling for a host if his guest has such a hangover that he can hardly face the day, but generally it will be a youth who has run in and quickly recovers on a Red Bull and some solids.

Lunch is a very key part of a shooting day and there are very firm views as to taking it at lunchtime or 'shooting through', and turning it into a longer affair after the last drive. On the Buccleuch moors in the 1970s I remember very happily that lunch was relatively sparse with soup, an egg and bacon bap and an apple. But it was light. There is now a fashion, both on the hill and down in the covers, to lay on these fantastic spreads. "You boys have been out there taking all that exercise in the cold," says the beaming hostess (or not so beaming depending on how many home days she has had to provide for!). So having already sunk an Olympique breakfast, a couple of Cumberlands at elevenses, you are now about to attack a vast Lake and Sidney, mash, and then a generous helping of Grannies leg, or treacle tart, cream etc…

The beaters may have stretched their legs and got a bit of cardiovascular going but the Guns, on the whole have done

Fit for all weathers.
From Shooting Types by Bryn Parry (Swan Hill Press)

absolutely nothing to burn off even a couple of hundred of the 3,000 calories already absorbed. Of course, we don't have to eat it all, but one has to be polite, and it's no fun picking at birdlike portions of rabbit food! Trouble is, big lunch means feeling a bit sleepy and you run the risk of losing that keen edge which is all-important to good performance. Sadly, the human body after a day or two of eating lots and taking no exercise, simply lays down pounds of fat. A year or two past there was a fine local squire who was bemoaning his corpulence to Ken who was mending his fence. After a moment's thought Ken (a lean sinewy man who has driven in a million fence posts by hand) delivered his solution: 'Aye Farmer, y'iv three options, man; eat less, shite mair, or burst.' True enough for many of us.

Perhaps we should aspire to be like a true Northumbrian, Colonel Bell, who turned 100 years old last year. He shot a driven grouse at Whitfield in the butts and caught a salmon on the fly at Countess Park on the Tyne, ghillied by my brother. Or General 'Dare' Wilson, aged 94, who caught three fish on the Exe in a morning, landing them all himself, and who I saw do up his shoelaces last year while standing on one leg. OK, these men will have a military austerity to their fitness and diet from their years in the army, but they are lean, relatively supple and carry themselves way better than many a 60-year-old.

I am in the mood for some nuts and seeds now, maybe some green gunk to drink and a few stretches. Even if it is a long time until the shooting season, perhaps a vaguely rigorous fitness regime and diet would clear the eye, prepare the heart and lungs and give speed and accuracy to one's shooting. After all, if you were about to play Roger Federer at Wimbledon, or compete in the Olympic Games would you train up or would you simply roll up all stiff and sweaty and make a bad job of it? What is more, if you go on to produce a string of awesome performances and generally do your duty, you may well become like José Mourinho, the 'special one', and find yourself supping at the table of the Gods.

It's worth
getting fit for.
Kirsten Scheuerl

CHAPTER THIRTEEN

Dangerous ground

THE MRS...

Man's love affair – or rather obsession – with his gun, fishing rods, his dogs, grouse, pigeons, rabbits, pheasants, trout, salmon, etc... is symbiotic with the changing seasons. Not of the sporting year, but of his partner's varying degrees of tolerance – a tolerance influenced by many different parameters and happiness or displeasure shown in myriad ways. Venturing to commentate about this is dangerous ground, but it's important to know why, just occasionally, our other halves might not send us out into the wilds quite as freely as we might wish.

To set the scene, first we have our young sportsman of say 15-years-old. Holidays long and short are filled with sporting adventure, and if he is fortunate and a little indulged there is no real restriction bar darkness, hunger or need for sleep. Even then, lamping bunnies or sea trouting are splendid

Braving the
elements (left) or
chasing winter sun?

Lab completing a
retrieve.
Simon Everett

The Power of the Dog

BY RUDYARD KIPLING

There is sorrow enough in the natural way
From men and women to fill our day;
And when we are certain of sorrow in store,
Why do we always arrange for more?
Brothers and Sisters, I bid you beware
Of giving your heart to a dog to tear.

Buy a pup and your money will buy
Love unflinching that cannot lie –
Perfect passion and worship fed
By a kick in the ribs or a pat on the head.
Nevertheless it is hardly fair
To risk your heart for a dog to tear.

When the fourteen years which Nature permits
Are closing in asthma, or tumour, or fits,
And the vet's unspoken prescription runs
To lethal chambers or loaded guns,
Then you will find – it's your own affair –
But...you've given your heart for a dog to tear.

When the body that lived at your single will,
With its whimper of welcome, is stilled (how still!);
When the spirit that answered your every mood
Is gone – wherever it goes – for good,
You will discover how much you care,
And will give your heart for the dog to tear.

We've sorrow enough in the natural way,
When it comes to burying Christian clay.
Our loves are not given, but only lent,
At compound interest of cent per cent.
Though it is not always the case, I believe,
That the longer we've kept 'em, the more do we grieve:
For, when debts are payable, right or wrong,
A short-time loan is as bad as a long –
So why in Heaven (before we are there)
Should we give our hearts to a dog to tear?

Cockers in
their element.
*Tarquin
Millington-Drake*

Index